DIAMONDS FROM THE SKY

A Parable By Wealthykids.org

Written by Shaana D Ramos
Illustration by Shaana D. Ramos/ Pictures by Thomas Mosley
ALL Rights reserved @ Copyright   Shaana D. Ramos for Wealthykids.org
Disclaimer

Published by Wealthykids.org
8175 Limonite Avenue Suite A
Riverside, CA 92509
sarahwealthinc@gmail.com

I0494140

GRAINS TO GROW ON

Entrepreneurship is hard work with lots of learning and Investment

Apprenticeship is

a learning   a skill from a master.

ENTREPRENEURSHIP is

"Apprenticed" by YOU,

Entrepreneurs,

You are your child's first teacher!

"Train up

The Child"

to Find THEIR

Story

Count The Cost !

Plan Ahead

Work Your Plan

Give Good Products And Services

A Word From Our Sponsor:
The Meaning of Diamonds In The Sky
Brought To You By
Pedez The Penguin And The Magic Ice Tray

All of Us Are In Business For God

He is The Master of our Apprenticeship

We Then pass on what we learn from
Our apprenticeship to others

God Trains us up,
His children and we train
our Children in the way
He says to go
for MUCH success !

*And
In ALL
Things
Do your
BEST,*

To Seek FIRST The Kingdom,

SunSet

And Let God Do The Rest.

FINI

WealthyKids.org

PEDEZ THE PENGUIN
AND THE MAGIC
ICE TRAY
A Parable By Wealthykids.org

Published by Wealthykids.org
8175 Limonite Avenue suite A
Riverside, CA 92509
sarahwealthinc@gmail.com